AXIS PARENT GUIDES SERIES

A PARENT'S GUIDE TO

SUICIDE & SELF-HARM PREVENTION

axis

Tyndale House Publishers
Carol Stream, Illinois

Visit Tyndale online at tyndale.com.

Tyndale and Tyndale's quill logo are registered trademarks of Tyndale House Ministries.

A Parent's Guide to Suicide & Self-Harm Prevention

For information about special discounts for bulk purchases, please contact Tyndale House Publishers at csresponse@tyndale.com, or call 1-855-277-9400.

Library of Congress Cataloging-in-Publication Data

A catalog record for this book is available from the Library of Congress.

ISBN 978-1-4964-6766-9

Printed in the United States of America

29	28	27	26	25	24	23
7	6	5	4	3	2	1

Anyone strong enough to kill himself is more than strong enough to live, ought to let himself live, and is very much needed among us.

JENNIFER HECHT, *STAY*

CONTENTS

A LETTER FROM AXIS

Dear Reader,

We're Axis, and since 2007, we've been creating resources to help connect parents, teens, and Jesus in a disconnected world. We're a group of gospel-minded researchers, speakers, and content creators, and we're excited to bring you the best of what we've learned about making meaningful connections with the teens in your life.

This parent's guide is designed to help start a conversation. Our goal is to give you enough knowledge that you're able to ask your teen informed questions about their world. For each guide, we spend weeks reading, researching, and interviewing parents and teens in order to distill everything you need to know about the topic at hand. We encourage you to read the whole thing and then to use the questions we include to get the conversation going with your teen—and then to follow the conversation wherever it leads.

As Douglas Stone, Bruce Patton, and Sheila Heen point out in their book *Difficult Conversations*, "Changes in attitudes and behavior rarely come about because of arguments, facts, and attempts to persuade. How often do *you* change your values and beliefs—or whom you love or what you want in life—based on something someone tells you? And how likely are you to do so when the person who is trying to change you doesn't seem fully aware of the reasons you see things differently in the first place?"[1] For whatever reason, when we believe that others are trying to understand *our* point of view, our defenses usually go down, and we're more willing to listen to *their* point of view. The rising generation is no exception.

So we encourage you to ask questions, to listen, and then to share your heart with your teen. As we often say at Axis, discipleship happens where conversation happens.

Sincerely,
Your friends at Axis

---

[1] Douglas Stone, Bruce Patton, and Sheila Heen, *Difficult Conversations: How to Discuss What Matters Most*, rev. ed. (New York: Penguin Books, 2010), 137.

YOU'RE NOT ALONE

LET'S ACKNOWLEDGE the elephant in the room: This is a scary topic that no parent wants to even *think* about. Which is completely understandable. After all, God created us for flourishing, abundant life, and relationship with Him, not pain, sadness, or the desire to no longer live.

Unfortunately, our broken world is full of dysfunction, disorder, and sin, all of which disrupt and decay the beautiful world God lovingly created for us. So what do we do when that reality hits home, when our children struggle with very real issues? How do we help our kids find physical, mental, emotional, and spiritual healing?

First, let us assure you that if you or a loved one is struggling, you're not alone. In 2020, there were an estimated 1.2 million suicide attempts in the US.[1] With the exception of accidents, suicide is the leading cause of death among young adults, teens, and children as young as age five, and 1 in 5 females and 1 in 7 males engage in some type of self-injury each year.[2]

But there is hope. Now more than ever, behavioral health providers are studying and learning about teen mental health issues, and new resources are created every year. God talks about it and deals with it directly in His Word. So, with deepest concern for your fears and sorrow for your struggles and losses, let's talk about it too.

AN IMPORTANT NOTE

THIS GUIDE HELPS PARENTS learn more about the troubling incidence of suicide and self-harm among young people. Like other parent guides in this series, it's a tool that provides knowledge, references, and faith-based encouragement on the subject to help parents connect with their kids. However, we do not pretend to be physicians, health-care providers, or even experts on these difficult matters. As such, this resource is *not* a substitute for medical advice or treatment. It can accompany and support steps recommended by a qualified health-care professional, but it is not meant to replace or preclude any diagnosis or treatment. Axis cannot be responsible for actions taken without professional medical guidance.

We cannot say it loud enough or often enough: **If you even suspect your child has suicidal thoughts or plans, STOP**

READING THIS AND TAKE ACTION NOW. Contact your family physician and tell them your teen is at risk of suicide and must be seen immediately. If a doctor cannot see them right away for whatever reason, do not leave your child alone until they can be seen and evaluated by a health-care professional qualified to assess adolescent behavioral health. If necessary, take your child to the nearest emergency room or urgent care center, demand priority, and do not leave the physician's office until next steps are in place (such as referral to a specialist, assessments, evaluations, treatment plans, outpatient/inpatient programs, etc.).

If you even suspect
your child has suicidal
thoughts or plans, STOP
READING THIS AND
TAKE ACTION NOW.

WHAT EXACTLY IS SUICIDE? SELF-HARM?

THE CENTERS FOR DISEASE CONTROL AND PREVENTION

define suicide as "death caused by injuring oneself with the intent to die."[3] The American Academy of Child & Adolescent Psychiatry reports that "the majority of children and adolescents who attempt suicide have a significant mental health disorder, usually depression."[4] In the very young, suicide attempts are often impulsive and can be triggered by feelings of sadness, confusion, anger, or problems with attention and hyperactivity. Among teens, suicide attempts may be associated with feelings of stress, self-doubt, pressure to succeed, financial uncertainty, disappointment, and loss.

Self-harm, clinically referred to as "non-suicidal self-injury" or NSSI, is defined as injury inflicted by a person on him/herself deliberately but without intent to die. Teens today often refer to self-harm as

THE HISTORY AND CULTURAL CONTEXT OF SUICIDE

"cutting" since the most common form of self-harm involves cutting the skin with a sharp object, such as a razor or knife. However, there are many forms of self-harm, including burning the skin with cigarettes or other hot objects, pulling hair, hitting oneself or banging one's body against walls, deep fingernail scratching, ingesting low levels of toxins, pinching the skin, or picking at wounds to prevent them from healing.[5]

Suicide is "death caused by injuring oneself with the intent to die."
—CDC

Self-harm is injury inflicted by a person on him/herself deliberately but without intent to die.

THE IDEA OF ENDING one's own life is certainly nothing new. For many years it has been visible (though not sanctioned) in US culture and even considered acceptable in other cultures. The ancient Greeks allowed convicted criminals to take their own lives; the ancient Romans did too, at first, until the high rate of suicide among slaves began to impact the wealth of slave-owners.[6] Some spiritual traditions (including Buddhism and Hinduism) see suicide as an acceptable option in particular situations. The concept of suicide appears frequently in visual art, literature, history books, film, and music from around the world. Terrorists and extremist religious groups consider suicide a valid option for the sake of causes they see as more significant than individual lives. Nine US states allow physician-assisted suicide for those suffering from terminal illnesses with a prognosis of fewer than six months to live.[7]

WHAT CAUSES SUICIDE OR SELF-HARM?

THERE ISN'T A SINGLE CAUSE for either behavior, and researchers are unsure what is causing the rates of both to increase. Some align the increase in screen time among teens with their rise in suicidal thoughts.[8] Others say bullying is the culprit.[9] Some point accusingly at today's parenting styles, some at a lack of awareness, and still others say it's because the world's values are falling apart.

There has also been speculation that exposure to graphic media is to blame. In March 2017, the independent television series *13 Reasons Why* explored a teen suicide in a more direct way than a series had ever dared before. The show focuses on a troubled high school student who records audio explanations of what and who influenced her decision to kill herself. Then she labels each tape with the name of a person (a total of thirteen, hence the title) she feels has contributed to the decision. Each episode of the show follows one of these people as they deal with the girl's self-inflicted death and the part they may have played in it. The first season originally ended with a brutal depiction of Hannah's suicide, though the scene was edited out by Netflix in 2019 on advice of suicide prevention experts. In season two, the students of Liberty High go through an emotional court-room trial connected to Hannah's death, while still dealing with their own issues, including sexual assault, self-harm, bul-lying, and gun violence. Season three is framed as a murder mystery, but it proved significantly less popular than the previ-ous two seasons.[10]

CNN reported that after the pilot episode aired, online search results for terms like "suicide," "suicide prevention," and "suicide awareness" rose significantly.[11] However, search results for the phrases "how to commit suicide" and "suicidal ideation" skyrocketed as well. Psychologists call this phenomenon "suicide contagion," when a group's exposure to details of a suicide result in increased suicidal behavior in that group. Horrifyingly, statistics show that if a struggling person sees suicide as a viable option, anything that triggers suicidal thoughts in that person can promote that belief and even advance it to the point of action.[12] In a panic, many schools and parent groups issued stern warnings to teens not to watch *13 Reasons Why* at all. Unfortunately, these warnings only served to amplify the message of the show, and teens' attention and conversation around suicide grew.

Dr. Victor Schwartz at the NYU School of Medicine explained that most teens—but not all—can watch shows like *13 Reasons Why* and walk away without suicidal thoughts or behaviors. However, he expressed real concern for young people watching the show who have a predilection for mental health problems or even existing problems that go undiagnosed.[13] These issues are, not surprisingly, known risk factors for suicide. Sadly, not all adults will consider mental illness as a possible reason for a teen's behavioral or emotional difficulty. That's one reason why only about a third of US adolescents with a diagnosable, treatable mental disorder ever receive treatment.[14] For some, sadly, critical help comes too late.

WHY WOULD SOMEONE ENGAGE IN SELF-HARM?

IF THE IDEA OF SELF-HARM makes you uncomfortable, you're not alone. Many assume self-harm signals the presence of a severe mental illness in a teen; after all, why else would someone intentionally hurt themselves?

Self-harming is not an illness in itself but rather points to a desperate situation and a dangerously severe inability to cope—which can be caused by one or any number of physical, mental, emotional, or spiritual issues. The urge to self-harm, like suicidal ideation, most often begins with overwhelming negative emotions and problems that seem unsolvable. Sometimes a person who continues to struggle with acute depression, emotional pain, or trauma will eventually "go numb": the brain can shut down emotions to protect itself from toxic levels of stress. This automatic neurological response can hold a person hostage inside themselves, preventing them from crying, getting angry, solving problems well, focusing, or even fully understanding what they feel and why.

In these frightening moments, self-harm can feel like a "release." Those who engage in it say they feel "real" and "alive" again because it makes their invisible, unexplainable pain visible. It can distract a person temporarily from the nonstop internal struggle they live with every day. A few even admit they self-harm in order to *stop* suicidal thoughts because the painful sensation briefly restores a sense of control over their lives.

Self-harming is not an illness in itself but rather points to a desperate situation and a dangerously severe inability to cope—which can be caused by one or any number of physical, mental, emotional, or spiritual issues.

HOW DOES CULTURE TREAT SUICIDE AND SELF-HARM? HOW DOES THAT INFLUENCE TEENS?

SUICIDE AND SELF-HARM are being portrayed in the media and talked about more openly than ever before. In some cases, as with National Suicide Prevention Week, this is a good thing.[15] In others, it's a mixed bag (see discussion above about *13 Reasons Why* and the impact it had).

One example of our culture's portrayal of suicide is Billie Eilish's music video "everything i wanted."[16] The Eilish-directed video is a chilling portrayal of a dream she had in which she committed suicide, and all her fans and friends turned their backs on her. Eilish then woke up from the dream to find her brother, Finneas, at her side, highlighting their close relationship. In the song, she describes herself stepping off the "Golden," that is, San Francisco's Golden Gate Bridge, a heartbreakingly popular site to commit suicide in the US. "Nobody cried," she sings. "Kinda thought they might care."

While your teen may not be able to connect with the fame aspect of these lyrics, many teenagers can relate to the feeling that their friends aren't *really* their friends. Sometimes it can be hard to tell who's on your side. That's why our kids need to be reassured daily of how much we love and care for them, that they've always got a listening ear, that they are cared for no matter what. We all need the reminder that our value and worth does not come from accomplishments but from our identity as children of God.

Perhaps the most notable occurrence of suicide references in our culture is the use of "You should kill yourself" or "Kill yourself" (often shortened as "kys" online) as an insult. A popular meme has also propagated the phrase.[17] The idea is to use it as a sarcastic response when someone does something completely inane or

We all need the
reminder that our
value and worth
does not come from
accomplishments but
from our identity as
children of God.

pathetic, with many online definitions clarifying that it's only meant sarcastically as a way to point out one's stupidity, not as an actual encouragement to kill oneself. The problems with this phrase are obvious: (1) It makes light of a very serious and heavy situation; (2) The recipient of such comments may not realize the sender is being sarcastic and therefore believe that others actually want them to commit suicide, as evidenced by this 15-year-old girl's suicide;[18] and (3) If the target of this phrase is already struggling with suicidal tendencies, it will only reinforce their desire to commit suicide.

Finally (though not exhaustively), many pro-suicide communities exist online. Subreddits like /r/kys and /r/SanctionedSuicide are places for users to submit questions about if, when, where, and how they should commit suicide, as well as to find "death partners." One study found that, between 2007 and 2014, the number of sites providing factual information about suicide methods had tripled.[19]

DO SOME TEENS THREATEN SUICIDE OR SELF-HARM TO GET ATTENTION OR MANIPULATE OTHERS?

IT'S PRETTY IMPORTANT THAT PARENTS FULLY understand the ramifications of this idea. As previously noted, suicidal ideation and self-harm both point to an inability to express or cope with intense feelings. Most often, a young person threatens or attempts these behaviors to relieve themselves of constant, unmanageable, unbearable emotional turmoil. Some teens see self-harm or suicide as their only solution, or they do it to beg for help with something they don't fully understand or have no words to describe. Sometimes they truly believe their feelings "don't matter" or they have failed at handling things on their own and feel ashamed (which makes matters worse).

Philosopher and author David Foster Wallace, who struggled with lifelong depression and eventually took his own life, described his desperation this way:

The . . . person who tries to kill
herself doesn't do so . . . because
death seems suddenly appealing.
The person in whom [an]
invisible agony reaches a certain
unendurable level will kill herself
the same way a trapped person
will eventually jump from the
window of a burning high-rise.
Make no mistake about people
who leap from burning windows.
Their terror of falling from a great
height is still just as great as it
would be for you or me standing
speculatively at the same window
just checking out the view; i.e., the
fear of falling remains a constant.
The variable here is the other
terror: the fire's flames. When the
flames get close enough, falling
to death becomes the slightly less
terrible of two terrors. . . . And yet

With the rate of teen suicide and self-harm rising, we can't afford to blow off our kids' efforts to be seen and heard, no matter how delinquent they may seem or how much we might fear we're to blame for it.

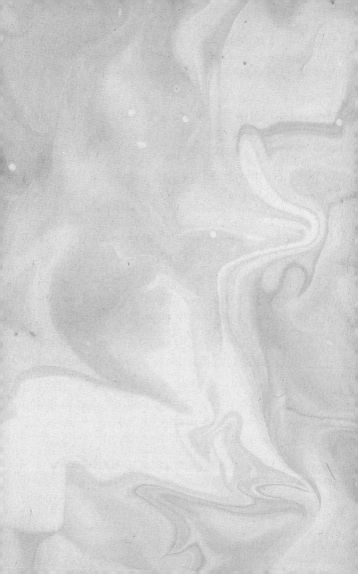

nobody down on the sidewalk, looking up and yelling "Don't!" and "Hang on!" can understand the jump. Not really. You'd have to have personally been trapped and felt flames to really understand a terror way beyond falling.[20]

Even on the outside chance your child's motivation is, in fact, to "get attention," maybe that attention is exactly what's needed. Threats, posturing, uncontrolled anger, isolation, misbehavior, disobedience . . . these are all symptoms in kids that should make us ask, "Why?" With the rate of teen suicide and self-harm rising, we can't afford to blow off our kids' efforts to be seen and heard, no matter how delinquent they may seem or how much we might fear we're to blame for it. Something serious is *always* behind this kind of behavior, and the real problem can get missed by parents who demand respect before giving it. We protect our teens and limit the "exasperation" factor (see Ephesians 6) when we make sure they aren't in severe emotional trouble before turning on the accusations. If there's truly no emotional danger, a few minutes of active listening will confirm it—you won't "spoil" your child or "enable" poor behavior in your teen by listening to them.

WHY DO SEEMINGLY HAPPY PEOPLE COMMIT SUICIDE OR HARM THEMSELVES?

MANY TEENS WHO HAVE SUICIDAL THOUGHTS or harm themselves are experts at hiding their pain—sometimes because they can't explain it well, sometimes because it doesn't make sense to them, and sometimes because they believe it is inappropriate, wrong, sinful, or dangerous to address it openly. Therefore, it's important to see beyond what a teen projects to what's really going on. These are some warning signs that your teen may be at risk of self-destructive behavior:

- Behavioral health concerns (mental illness, substance abuse, learning difficulties)

- Personality characteristics (low self-esteem, loneliness, social isolation or exclusion, low tolerance for stress, poor coping skills or body image)

- Adverse circumstances (death of a loved one, interpersonal difficulties, disciplinary or legal problems, abuse, trauma, serious illness)

- Unwise lifestyle choices (alcohol/ drug use, delinquency, aggressive/ violent behavior, sexual activity)

- Family history (suicide or self-harm, mental illness, parental divorce or marriage difficulties, financial problems, over/underprotective or highly critical parents)

- Environmental factors (negative experiences at school, lack of respect or acceptance of differences at home or school, limited safety at school, weapons present on campus, limited access to mental health care, exposure to stigma or discrimination)

Many teens who have
suicidal thoughts or harm
themselves are experts
at hiding their pain—
sometimes because they
can't explain it well ... and
sometimes because they
believe it is inappropriate,
wrong, sinful, or dangerous
to address it openly.

WHAT STEPS CAN I TAKE TO HELP PREVENT SUICIDE OR SELF-HARM?

EVEN WITH THIS WIDE VARIETY of risk factors, powerful defensive measures exist. Studies on teen incidence of suicide and self-harm suggest ways to prevent and even heal the issues leading to these tragic outcomes. If any of the following descriptions are true of your teen, they will be less likely to harm themselves.

- Having a strong set of core values based in a growing faith in Christ

- Going through intentional positive reinforcement and emotional self-care training

- Possessing emotional intelligence, adaptability, resilience, self-discipline, and good coping and problem-solving skills

- Possessing a sense of agency, self-esteem, frustration tolerance, and healthy body image

- Getting regular exercise

- Participating in school groups like sports and music

- Receiving familial and social support (parental involvement, demonstrated active listening skills, family closeness, availability of friends and other caring adults, emphasis on school success, the modeling and approval of socially healthy behavior)

- Having access to effective health care

- Being in a safe school community where young people feel valued, heard, and successful

- Lacking access to weapons, alcohol, and drugs

HOW CAN I KNOW IF MY CHILD IS SUICIDAL AND/OR SELF-HARMING?

***ANY ONE* OF THE FOLLOWING BEHAVIORS** could indicate your child is at risk of suicide and needs intervention:

- Talk or social media interaction about suicide or wanting to die (that, to your parental instincts, sounds like more than normal teenage hyperbole)

- Evidence of a suicide plan (such as an online search history, the obtaining of a weapon, or a stockpile of over-the-counter medications)

- Talk of feeling hopeless, having no reason to live, feeling trapped, feeling they are a burden to others, or experiencing unbearable pain, fear, or trouble (emotional or physical)

- Statements like "You won't have to worry about me for much longer" or "Soon all my troubles will be over." (They might even begin to give away some of their belongings.)

- Increasing use of drugs or alcohol, including over-the-counter medications

- Increasingly risky, reckless behavior

- Easily induced agitation or rage

- Frequent sleep disturbances (too much, too little, nightmares)

- Isolation or withdrawal, especially from people or activities they used to enjoy

- Increasingly rapid and/or extreme mood swings

Remember the notice at the beginning of this guide! **If you even suspect your child has suicidal thoughts or plans, STOP READING AND TAKE ACTION NOW.**

The following symptoms may indicate the presence of self-harming behavior:

- Clusters of scars, cuts, scratches, or burns on the wrists, hands, or forearms (although those who self-harm may choose any place on their body)

- Frequent bruising or use of bandages

- Hair loss or bald patches on the scalp

- Isolation or withdrawal

- Wearing long sleeves, pants, or wristbands in hot weather

- Claiming frequent accidents or mishaps resulting in injury

HOW CAN I GET MY TEEN TO TALK WITH ME ABOUT THESE ISSUES?

TRY STARTING WITH ONE OR MORE OF THESE CONVERSATION OPENERS:

- "Tell me more about what's happening to you. I'm here to listen."

- "How are you feeling? Have you felt like this before?"

- "I'm worried about you. It looks like you're going through a difficult time." (Then list the behaviors you've observed.)

- "I care. I want to listen and understand. What do you want me to know about the way you feel and what's going on?"

- "Can you talk to me about what you're experiencing? Do you want to talk to someone else about this? Who might that be?"

- "How can I help you feel better?"

- "What else can I help you with?"

- "Who/What helps you deal with this?"

- "Do you know anyone else who has experienced these issues?"

- "How can I help you find the support you need?"

- "Do you ever have thoughts of harming yourself?"

Begin the conversation when and where your teen feels safe, comfortable, and calm (not during or right after a conflict). Seek first to listen actively and gain as much insight from them as possible. Be straightforward and honest about what you see, how it makes you feel, and why you are worried. Watch for reactions in your teen. If they start to recoil or appear confused or upset, slow down or back up and try another approach.

If your teen admits to self-harming, suicidal ideation, or even planning suicide, take a deep breath and don't panic. Tell them you are there to help them. Verbally commit to doing whatever is necessary to get them any help they need, and be prepared to reiterate that commitment whenever your teen has questions. Explain specifically how you will take action: "I will call your doctor right now and get an appointment to talk about this." "I will get a referral to a doctor who specializes in helping young people." "I will get a referral to a doctor who specializes in what you're experiencing and feeling."

If your teen admits to self-harming, suicidal ideation, or even planning suicide, take a deep breath and don't panic. Tell them you are there to help them.

WHAT DOES GOD'S WORD SAY ABOUT SUICIDE AND SELF-HARM?

IN 1 KINGS, THE PROPHET ELIJAH orchestrated one of God's most visible, effective, and dramatic victories: God sent fire to consume a huge pile of soaking-wet rocks and about a thousand false prophets on top of Mount Carmel in front of a teeming horde of lukewarm Israelites. Elijah, with immovable faith, even harassed the Baal prophets because they weren't getting answers to their prayers: "Hey! You should pray louder! You said he's gotta be there, right? Maybe he's multitasking, or maybe he's taking a nap! Maybe he's on a road trip or something!" These Baal guys actually "slashed themselves with swords and spears" until they were "covered in blood" in a desperate effort to protect their livelihood—and their lives (see 1 Kings 18:16-41). Fear, pride, shame, disillusion, pretty much any separation from God's purpose can clearly make people do desperate things to cope.

Immediately afterward, in 1 Kings 19, with this amazing spiritual victory fresh in his mind, Elijah wandered out into the desert, collapsed under a tree, and told God he was ready to die. The idol-worshiping queen swore to kill Elijah because he had made her look ridiculous. Despite Elijah's world-famous, unwavering faith, exhaustion and fear for his life overwhelmed him. At that point, death represented eternity with God and seemed much more desirable than hanging out on earth with people in authority positions who had unlimited resources and were trying to kill him.

God responded to his servant by first providing for Elijah's most immediate needs—food, water, and rest—because "the journey was too much" for him (1 Kings 19:7). Those needs were fulfilled with God's own messenger: he sent an angel who touched Elijah (he didn't need to, but he knew it would be soothing to him), he made him a fresh breakfast, and he even placed the food near Elijah's head so he wouldn't have to move too far to reach it. The angel stayed with Elijah and fed him twice as he rested and restored his soul in the presence of God. (Renowned missionary Mother Teresa also focused first on the most basic needs of the poor and frail while she prayed over them. In Christlikeness, she understood the delicate and vital interplay between our physical, mental, emotional, and spiritual health—especially among the more com-promised children of God.)

Strengthened and rested, Elijah then traveled forty days into the desert to meet with the Father on his own mountain, Mt. Horeb. God told Elijah, "Go out and stand before me on the mountain" (19:11). Three powerful forces shattered the earth around Elijah, but he knew God well enough to keep waiting.

God came tenderly to Elijah "in a gentle whisper" (19:12) likely because He knew Elijah had stressed enough. The Father then asked him, "What are you doing here, Elijah?" (19:13)—not for His own benefit but so Elijah could talk about what was frightening him to the point of irrationality (a biblical example of "talk therapy"). Elijah told God how hard he'd worked, the rejection he'd experienced from the people he was sent to save, the frustrating behavior of those lost people, what had happened to every other prophet God sent to them (it wasn't good), that he was all alone in the world, and how evil, idol-worshiping authority figures were trying to have him murdered.

God's response this time? "Go back."

What?! We think at first something must be wrong . . . then we continue to read. God sent Elijah back home with everything he

[God's Word highlights what] every struggling teen (and adult, for that matter) needs in times of life-threatening emotional crisis: personalized care, a listening ear, mercy, guidance, a glimpse of the big picture, and deep personal healing based in love and respect for our shared human condition.

was missing: direction, authority, a partner and successor in the good work (Elisha), people who would be faithful to God and obedient to Elijah, and reassurance of the Father's personal presence through it all. God didn't just heal Elijah—He *heard* him. God gave Elijah comfort, purpose, power, strength, protection, fellowship, and the renewed promise to never leave him. Best of all, He showed up.

This passage illustrates vividly what every struggling teen (and adult, for that matter) needs in times of life-threatening emotional crisis: personalized care, a listening ear, mercy, guidance, a glimpse of the big picture, and deep personal healing based in love and respect for our shared human condition. Even more importantly, suffering people need Christ to give them these things. The Great Physician is able to heal us in every way we can be healed in His perfect timing.

FINAL THOUGHTS

WHEN WE DISCOVER SUICIDE and self-harm as part of our children's reality, it sets off an emotional whirlwind: "How did this happen?" "Is it my fault?" "What do I say?" "What if it's too late to help?" "How did I not notice it before?" There's fear, worry, panic, confusion, disgust, embarrassment, anger, frustration . . . and the list goes on. It's hard to deal with our own feelings, figure out a game plan, and implement that plan when the stakes are so incredibly high. *However, remember that suicide and self-harm are usually preventable* (except possibly when severe mental health issues are present), *and good treatment can provide incredible peace, improve quality of life exponentially for struggling teens, and bond families together like never before.*

The most important thing you can do to help a suicidal or self-harming teen is to *be there*. Have compassion, actively listen, and do whatever's necessary to implement a healthy solution, even if it means a long season of hunting down the right health-care providers, treatment plans, inpatient care, support systems, and coping strategies.

And don't forget to *get the right support for yourself*. As much as your struggling teen needs your intervention and guidance, you need encouragement to keep fighting the good fight alongside them.

Suicide and self-harm are not unforgivable sins (despite what you may have heard), but God never wants them to enter and hijack the abundant life for which He made us. Pray often and fervently for His provision, grant Him daily control over the situation, and allow Him to work in unexpected ways. As Christ

Remember that suicide
and self-harm are usually
preventable (except
possibly when severe
mental health issues
are present), and good
treatment can provide
incredible peace, improve
quality of life exponentially
for struggling teens, and
bond families together like
never before.

has "overcome the world" (John 16:33), rest assured He can work all things for good (Romans 8:28), even this.

Pastor and author Tim Keller writes in *Walking with God through Pain and Suffering*: "Christianity teaches that . . . suffering is meaningful. There is a purpose to it, and if faced rightly, it can drive us like a nail deep into the love of God and into more stability and spiritual power than you can imagine."[21]

RECAP

- **If you even suspect your child has suicidal thoughts or plans, stop reading this and take action now.**

- As heartbreaking as it is, suicide and self-harm are very real and prevalent issues in youth culture today.

- Among teens, suicide attempts may be associated with feelings of stress, depression, self-doubt, disappointment, and loss.

- There are many forms of self-harm, including cutting, burning the skin with cigarettes or other hot objects, pulling hair, and hitting oneself or banging one's body against walls.

- There are many speculations as to what causes suicide or self-harm, including bullying, faulty parenting values, and exposure to graphic media or internet content.

- Suicide and self-harm tend to be viewed as means to cope and get release from emotional turmoil in someone's life.

- Even if you would never expect your child to have suicidal or self-harming tendencies, it is important to look for warning signs such as risky behaviors, personality changes, and concerning statements.

- Being intentional with your children relationally, emotionally, and spiritually—as well as setting a positive example and having a strong family support system—can help prevent conditions that lead to these issues.

- Having honest and open conversations with your child about how they are doing can be a successful gateway to talking about suicide and self-harm.

- If your child expresses suicidal thoughts or admits to self-harm, it is important not to panic or lash out at them but rather to make sure they know you are there for them and willing to do whatever it takes to help.

DISCUSSION
QUESTIONS

1. Have you or anyone you know ever struggled with suicidal thoughts? An urge to self-harm? What did you or they do to deal with it?

2. How do your friends talk about mental health issues? Do you have someone besides me that you can talk to if you're struggling?

3. How do you feel when talking about mental health?

4. Do you wish I talked about mental health more often or differently? If so, how and why?

5. What's something you wish I knew about your mental health?

6. What does the Bible say about our broken world? How does it teach us to deal with the brokenness we see or feel?

7. How can you better help those who have mental health struggles? Do you know what to do if a friend tells you they're considering self-harm or suicide?

8. How can I best help you press into God during your dark times?

ADDITIONAL RESOURCES

1. National Suicide Prevention Lifeline, https://988lifeline.org/ or call 988

2. Suicide Awareness Voices of Education (SAVE), https://save.org/ or call 988

3. To Write Love on Her Arms, https://twloha.com/

4. Saddleback Church's "Mental Health Resource Guide for Individuals and Families," http://www.mentalhealth ministries.net/resources/resource _guides/Hope_Resource_Guide.pdf

5. Mental Health Ministries, http://www .mentalhealthministries.net/

6. *Christianity Today*'s "Top 10 Resources for Mental Health Ministry," https://www .christianitytoday.com/pastors/2016/april -web-exclusives/top-10-resources-for -mental-health-ministry.html

7. American Psychiatric Association, https:// www.apa.org/

8. Centers for Disease Control and Prevention, https://www.cdc.gov/suicide/facts/index.html?CDC_AA_refVal=https%3A%2F%2Fwww.cdc.gov%2Fviolenceprevention%2Fsuicide%2Ffastfact.html

9. World Health Organization, https://www.who.int/en/news-room/fact-sheets/detail/suicide

10. Video, "How to Tell When a Kid Is Struggling Emotionally," https://www.youtube.com/watch?v=xJISfSma-0w

11. Video, "Stories of Hope and Recovery: Glenn Close," https://www.youtube.com/watch?v=zMdFj4e0Q18

NOTES

1. "Suicide Statistics," American Foundation for Suicide Prevention, accessed October 3, 2022, https://afsp.org/suicide-statistics/.

2. "About Suicide," Suicide Prevention Resource Center, accessed September 21, 2022, https://www.sprc.org/about-suicide; Samantha Gluck, "Self Injury, Self Harm Statistics and Facts," HealthyPlace, accessed September 21, 2022, https://www.healthyplace.com/abuse/self-injury/self-injury-self-harm-statistics-and-facts.

3. "Facts about Suicide," CDC, accessed September 21, 2022, https://www.cdc.gov/suicide/facts/index.html?CDC_AA_refVal=https%3A%2F%2Fwww.cdc.gov%2Fviolenceprevention%2Fsuicide%2Ffastfact.html.

4. "Suicide in Children and Teens," American Academy of Child & Adolescent Psychiatry, June 2021, https://www.aacap.org//AACAP/Families_and_Youth/Facts_for_Families/FFF-Guide/Teen-Suicide-010.aspx.

5. Deborah Serani, "Depression and Non-Suicidal Self Injury," *Psychology Today*,

February 28, 2012, https://www
.psychologytoday.com/us/blog/two-takes
-depression/201202/depression-and-non
-suicidal-self-injury.

6. "Suicide," Britannica, August 22, 2022, https://
   www.britannica.com/topic/suicide.

7. "Physician-Assisted Suicide Fast Facts," CNN,
   May 26, 2022, https://www.cnn.com/2014
   /11/26/us/physician-assisted-suicide-fast
   -facts/index.html.

8. Jean M. Twenge, "Have Smartphones
   Destroyed a Generation?" *Atlantic*, September
   2017, https://www.theatlantic.com/magazine
   /archive/2017/09/has-the-smartphone
   -destroyed-a-generation/534198/.

9. "Bullying and Suicide," Bullying Statistics,
   accessed September 21, 2022, http://www
   .bullyingstatistics.org/content/bullying-and
   -suicide.html.

10. Constance Grady, "There Are Zero Reasons
    Why *13 Reasons Why* Season 3 Should Exist,"
    Vox, August 31, 2019, https://www.vox.com
    /culture/2019/8/31/20840722/13-reasons-why
    -season-3-review.

11. Jacqueline Howard, "'13 Reasons Why' Tied to Rise in Suicide Searches Online," CNN Health, July 31, 2017, https://www.cnn.com/2017/07/31 /health/13-reasons-why-suicide-study/index.html.

12. "What Does 'Suicide Contagion' Mean, and What Can Be Done to Prevent It?" HHS.gov, February 25, 2019, https://www.hhs.gov /answers/mental-health-and-substance -abuse/what-does-suicide-contagion-mean /index.html.

13. Howard, "'13 Reasons Why' Tied to Rise in Suicide Searches Online."

14. Kathleen Ries Merikangas et al., "Service Utilization for Lifetime Mental Disorders in U.S. Adolescents: Results of the National Comorbidity Survey—Adolescent Supplement (NCS-A), *Journal of the American Academy of Child & Adolescent Psychiatry* 50, no. 1 (January 1, 2011): 32–45, https://www.ncbi .nlm.nih.gov/pmc/articles/PMC4408275/.

15. Krystal Jagoo, "How to Recognize National Suicide Prevention Week," Verywell Mind, September 27, 2022, https://www.verywellmind .com/national-suicide-prevention-week -6503932.

16. Billie Eilish, "everything i wanted," YouTube, video, 4:47, January 23, 2020, https://www.youtube.com/watch?v=EgBJmlPo8Xw.

17. "Kill Yourself," Know Your Meme, accessed September 21, 2022, https://knowyourmeme.com/memes/kill-yourself.

18. Elizabeth Chuck, "Is Social Media Contributing to Rising Teen Suicide Rate?" NBC News, October 22, 2017, https://www.nbcnews.com/news/us-news/social-media-contributing-rising-teen-suicide-rate-n812426?inf_contact_key=4418efd207b3e705ba71b3535876090eeb3f7f487409a6cc8289fa92b0182b88.

19. Nathaniel P. Morris, "'Pro-Suicide' Websites Lure Too Many People," *Chicago Tribune*, April 24, 2017, https://www.chicagotribune.com/lifestyles/health/ct-pro-suicide-websites-lure-too-many-people-20170424-story.html.

20. Bruce Weber, "David Foster Wallace, Influential Writer, Dies at 46," *New York Times*, September 14, 2008, https://www.nytimes.com/2008/09/15/books/15wallace.html.

21. Timothy Keller, *Walking with God through Pain and Suffering* (New York: Riverhead Books, 2013), 30.

PARENT GUIDES TO SOCIAL MEDIA
BY AXIS

It's common to feel lost in your teen's world. Let these be your go-to guides on social media, how it affects your teen, and how to begin an ongoing conversation about faith that matters.

BUNDLE THESE 5 BOOKS AND SAVE

PARENT GUIDES TO FINDING TRUE IDENTITY
BY AXIS

When culture is constantly pulling teens away from Christian values, let these five parent guides spark an ongoing conversation about finding your true identity in Christ.

BUNDLE THESE 5
BOOKS AND SAVE